The Wesleyan Way

How to Build a Championship High School Soccer Program

MICHAEL ZIGARELLI

CONTENTS

INTRODUCTION

A HISTORY OF HARDWARE

Fall 2002. A year before he took the head coaching position at Wesleyan Christian Academy, Scott Reitnour watched incredulously as a Wesleyan player warmed up before a match sporting a massive clown wig. A few weeks later he witnessed another warning sign: Wesleyan bowed out in the first round of the post-season. Worse still, most of the guys were indifferent after the match. Even the seniors. No tears, no remorse. Just a collective shrug.

The former dynasty that was Wesleyan boys' soccer had clearly lost its indomitable edge. Four head coaches in the past four years had taken its fatal toll on the culture.

Fast forward to the end of the 2003 season, Reitnour's first. Wesleyan again dropped its first-round playoff game, but this time there wasn't a dry eye on the bench. The seniors were especially devastated. On the bus ride home, the team approached Reitnour with a rogue request: "Coach, can we have one more practice tomorrow?" It was from the heart. Nobody wanted it to end. He gladly complied.

The next year, Wesleyan would be the state runner-up; the following year, they'd win it all. The drought dating back to 1998 was over; the Men of Troy were hoisting the North Carolina trophy once again.

Despite the hiatus, Wesleyan's numbers are staggering. Since 1984—33 seasons—the Wesleyan boys' team has been to the state title match 21 times, claiming 14 championships. That heap of hardware puts them in some pretty exclusive company among U.S. high school programs, many of them more lavishly resourced. Few even come close.

So how do they do it? Call it "The Wesleyan Way." It's a systematic method that anyone can imitate in pursuit of breakthrough results. This monograph reveals 12 secrets of their success.

But first, let's be clear on what it's not. Wesleyan's soccer program does not have any discernable budget or facility advantages when compared to most of their rivals. The school is not relatively larger in size; instead, they've often been smaller than their competition, advancing from 1A to 2A to 3A over this period. And except for their early years, the program's success has not come from talent transferring to the school.

Rather, the real and replicable drivers are deeper and more intangible—issues like purpose, leadership, culture and clever training methodologies. We'll begin with their cornerstone.

PRINCIPLE 1

PURSUE A PURPOSE BIGGER THAN WINNING

It's a paradox. Focusing on something other than winning soccer games can help you win more soccer games. It can't be just anything, though. It has to be a purpose that supercharges everyone in a way that a mere scoreboard or trophy cannot.

Legendary coach John Wooden consistently claimed: "I never mentioned winning." Seldom do the coaches at Wesleyan Christian Academy mention it either. Instead, their overriding, supercharging purpose is their middle name. More specifically, the primary mission has long been to honor God by developing "men built for others."

That's instilled in countless ways, from daily instruction to, more powerfully, the seniors cleaning the bus after road trips to the consistent role modeling by the servant-leader coaches. They also tap players and coaches from faith-based college and professional soccer programs (e.g., the Charlotte Eagles, Messiah College, Southern Wesleyan University, Eastern University) who credibly reaffirm this message of selflessness.

Soccer results are a byproduct. To take just a small example, a "men built for others" mindset inspires the right wing to sprint 60 yards—without hesitation or complaint or need for recognition—to cover for his overlapping defender. On the next possession, it prompts him to play a seven ball rather than hit a low percentage shot. Later in the match it allows him to give up his spot graciously so the second unit can train for the future.

Multiply those small choices by a thousand over a season and Wesleyan wins games that they may have lost otherwise. It's not so much "team over individual" as it is "you over me," a rare and relational disposition that gets guys ready to die for one another.

The mindset also explains the extraordinary time invested by the coaches—themselves men built to serve the boys and one another—coaches who far outwork their peers and their paychecks. Watch for that commitment in these next performance principles.

PRINCIPLE 2

HIRE OVER-QUALIFIED COACHES WHO NEVER STOP LEARNING

David Sanford, the Wesleyan boys' coach from 1981 to 1998, has a distinctive soccer pedigree: Taught to play soccer by Anson Dorrance, mentored to coach by Hank Steinbrecher—in a way, it's no surprise that Sanford eventually earned the NSCAA National Coach of the Year award and a spot in the North Carolina Coaching Hall of Fame. And as he took the team from a few names on a sign-up sheet in 1981 to a state title in 1984 to 13 state final appearances (winning nine of those) and a couple top-ten national rankings during his career, he had plenty of opportunities for more prestigious, more lucrative positions. But the over-qualified Dorrance-disciple remained at Wesleyan, building a team into a program into a benchmark.

His handpicked successor did not sign on until five years after Sanford left, but when he did, Coach Scott Reitnour proved he was the right man for the reboot.

He's now led the Wesleyan boys for 14 seasons, boasting Sanford-like numbers of his own: Eight appearances in the state finals, five championships, a top-three national ranking thrice. And as a three-time finalist for NSCAA National Coach of the Year award, Reitnour is clearly as under-employed as Sanford was.

But the leadership acumen doesn't end there. Wisely, both Sanford and Reitnour recruited high-level assistants. That's no small task when the money isn't remotely commensurate with the assistants' soccer IQ. Reitnour now talks of his staff as "an elite class of soccer coaches who could clearly run high school programs elsewhere and even coach at the college level." At some home matches there's a veritable entourage of eight paid and volunteer coaches—truth-tellers, not yes-men—flanking the bench.

This also explains the coaching staff's success: Their capabilities have never degenerated into complacency. Quite the opposite, they've been in perpetual learning mode, earning NSCAA diplomas, borrowing heavily from other programs, devouring soccer and leadership books on their own and alongside the team. Sanford describes himself as "a voracious student of the game," an apprenticeship that took him all the way to Holland in the 1990s to study the Dutch game with Assistant Coach Kevin Barrows (who himself earned the NSCAA Assistant Coach of the Year award in 2012). Reitnour, for his part, in addition to the incessant cutting and pasting, regularly brings in top-flight coaches and pro players to his training sessions to teach both him and his team. His basic posture could be a leadership mantra: "Humble yourself. Bring people into the program who are better than you. It won't demean, devalue or diminish your strengths."

In fact, it will make over-qualified coaches and over-achieving teams even better.

BUILD THE BEST ENVIRONMENT IN THE STATE TO PLAY SOCCER

It was a new coach's nightmare, but David Sanford turned it into an opportunity. Only six boys signed-up to play for Wesleyan in 1981, his inaugural season. So he went classroom to classroom, cobbling together a team by recruiting athletic-looking boys, most of them basketball players. Both that season and the next, Sanford basically ran a full-season soccer camp, just trying to achieve a respectable level of play.

But a funny thing happened on the road to respectability. Soccer studs from other schools started migrating to Wesleyan Christian. Word had gotten out about a coach with high standards and technical know-how who, curiously, also cared about his boys as *people* rather than as *players*. Coach Sanford was crafting the kind of demanding yet nurturing culture that select players quietly crave. The internal payoff was an increasingly talented and cohesive team; the external payoff was a state title in

1984 and then a reign of seven titles over eight years, beginning in 1988.

Sanford's theory resonates: Cultivate an attractive soccer environment and the kids will come running. Three decades later, the theory remains and the environment is better than ever. Two hundred rowdy students fill the stands at a typical Wesleyan home game, including many wide-eyed grade schoolers with noses pressed to the fence. It's a bigger crowd than most of these players will see even in their college careers.

"We have a rich soccer culture," explains Coach Reitnour. "If you lived with us for a year, you'd say 'they never stop doing soccer stuff.'"

That's benchmarking gold right there: Construct a 12-month program, not a three-month program. Make soccer relevant and cool all year long. Energize the community through victories in-season and soccer-related events out-of-season. To become state champions, build the best environment in the state to play soccer.

How? Here's a peek behind the red-and-black curtain (see Appendix F for a longer look). In January, they sponsor an indoor tournament, overflowing with 50+ teams of Wesleyan students and soccer alums. In February there's a tournament for everyone else—a competition for "non-athletic regular people" in the Wesleyan community, smartly packaged as "NARP Fest"—where hundreds of parents, teachers, staff and current players come together on mixed teams to crown an annual "King of the Court." Throughout the spring, the varsity team runs an instructional league for elementary school kids, the "Wesleyan Instructional Soccer League," beckoning with the fortuitous acronym WISL. They do it again as a week-long summer camp.

More informally, many varsity players eat lunch together daily in the coach's classroom, building brick-by-brick what Reitnour calls Wesleyan's "relationship crucible"—part of how boys become "men built for others." And pulling it all together, quite inventively, is their annual highlight video, premiering with breathless fanfare at a sports banquet in May. Filmed and produced with Madison Avenue polish by Assistant Coach Harry Sherwood, it recaps the year for players, parents and posterity, reinforcing the "rich soccer culture" that undergirds Wesleyan Christian.

PRINCIPLE 4

TRAIN THE VARSITY
FROM KINDERGARTEN

What if an American high school program created its own youth academy? How much of a competitive advantage would it enjoy?

Whereas the 1980s and 90s saw success through special players attracted to an environment, Wesleyan talent during the past two decades has been primarily home-grown. First, there's the aforementioned and acclaimed "WISL program"—after-school instruction in the spring that introduces the elementary school kids to the technical skills and principles of play of the varsity program. Think "two-touch, pass and sprint, a three-touch Cruyff option, one touch in transition" ... in third grade.

The goal? According to the varsity coach, whose players run the WISL sessions: "It creates kids who will matriculate into the middle school program with a foundation for what we're going to do there, and so on to the

JV program and to the varsity program. It's not completely like a European youth academy; it's also a place to simply attract kids to soccer, build community, train them in the basics of the program, and identify and encourage talent."

Launched in 1995 by Coaches Sanford and Barrows, and then accelerated by Coach Reitnour in the mid-2000s, at least three-quarters of the varsity players the past several years have been WISL trainees.

And the upshot? Reitnour is adamant: "It's been vital for maintaining continuity and earning Final Four appearances in the state tournament. If you don't have that player development underneath, what you're relying on is what everybody else relics on—the athletic group coming through, or that random pocket of kids who all started playing club together comes through. But we're gonna be good year in and year out because there's a constant drip of developed soccer talent."

Now, instead of teams with patchy quality like they had early on, relying on a few guys to get them through, Wesleyan's varsity consistently has more than 20 quality players, with a second unit capable of beating the first unit. The home-grown approach has been nothing if not ingeniously intentional.

So too has been their "Wesleyan Wednesdays" training. The principle is the same: high-level training for younger players, led by the varsity, preparing the former to become the latter. Unlike WISL, they conduct this *in-season*, every Wednesday afternoon in the fall, combining the middle school, JV and varsity boys (that is, grades 6-

12) using a "pool training" approach. That's more than 90 kids on the field simultaneously, across eight stations, "with all of the exercises fitting stylistically how we're ultimately trying to play," according to Coach Reitnour.

And there's an inexorable efficiency to it all. They use the scoreboard to show how much time is left at each station and they use a microphone to move everyone along. Kids sprint from one station to the next. Then, once they've completed the circuit, they move to conditioned, small-sided games with integrated teams—the twelfth grader alongside the freshman and the middle schooler—with the final 10 minutes of the day devoted to "sports ministry training," varsity leaders teaching a lesson to their mentees about character development or core values.

The details of their prolific pipeline are worth a closer look. They're unpacked in Appendices A, B and C.

PRINCIPLE 5

GIVE THEM THE KEYS BUT
HOLD THEM ACCOUNTABLE

"It was the best coaching decision I ever made." David Sanford stands by that statement to this day.

In 1993, a spate of injuries mutated into an unprecedented five-game losing streak. The capstone was a particularly unappealing performance in a mid-season tournament. The 5-1 smoking by Charlotte Country Day was the worst defeat ever for a Sanford squad.

It was also their first year stepping up from 1A to 2A. Bigger schools, bigger challenges. The biggest, though, was internal: a team that wasn't responding to anything the now-veteran coach had to say. So Sanford tasked a couple team leaders with this edict: "Meet with your team and decide what you want to do with this season. I'm not going to fight you anymore. If you guys want to pack it in, we'll just finish out the season."

It was an enormous gamble, but one that's consistent with the Wesleyan philosophy of player empowerment. Sanford is didactic about it: "I never scored a goal for Wesleyan; I never made a save. These guys had to decide what they really wanted for their team."

The forty-minute player meeting yielded one concise objective: "Coach, we want to win the state championship." Assuming this was a quixotic quest to prove their manhood, Sanford pushed back: "Don't BS me." But there was a resolve. Sanford could see it in their eyes, so he relented: "Fine, but you have to keep yourselves accountable to that goal. Let's get to work."

It was an inflection point. The '93 Wesleyan team did not lose another game that year, regular or postseason. And in cherry-on-top fashion, the state final was a clean sheet victory over Charlotte Country Day.

Owning the objective helped them own the competition. Current Coach Scott Reitnour ascribes to the same philosophy. He literally hands over a set of keys to the seniors at the beginning of each season, symbolizing their ownership (Wesleyan's preferred term is "stewardship") of the program. It's an entrustment that elevates 17-year-olds beyond themselves. Players rise to the level of excellence expected of them.

But also like his predecessor, Reitnour insists on accountability. He's built an entire culture around it. One example, but there are dozens: The boys do fitness testing not just in pre-season, but in November, January and May. Set the treadmill to 12.0 and go for as long as you can. And the results get posted on the coach's classroom door for the whole world to see.

Think you're good because you're at the top of the

list? Reitnour pulls out the historical record. "This guy in 2008 went a full three minutes longer than you did. That's your new standard."

Nobody blinks at that sort of reframing. Accountability is a way of life here—to the program, to the coaches, to one's teammates, ultimately to the Higher Standard that is their core mission. Without "deep accountability," as Reitnour calls it, no one would be writing or reading about Wesleyan soccer.

PRINCIPLE 6

GET AWAY DURING THE PRE-SEASON

Wesleyan has, for 30 years, brought collegiate level pre-season prep to the high school game—two-a-days, three-a-days, warm-ups at 8 a.m., book discussions at 8 p.m. It builds chemistry and skills while allowing them to unpack every drill and set piece they'll use through November.

Traditionally, a staple has also been getting out of town. It's simply transformational. Coach Sanford usually took his teams to a lake retreat, sometimes having to fundraise to pull it off. "It got them away from their girlfriends and intensified our focus. We'd get them up at dark-o-clock and go for a run. We'd have multiple trainings each day, often with guest coaches who would run it at a high level. But we also did things completely unrelated to soccer—team building, competitive games in the lake, talent contests, crazy stuff."

More recently, getting "away" in pre-season has meant an overnight at the school, deferring their out of town trip till September to play top-quality competition. "You have to get on the road once a year, if you have the means," insists Coach Reitnour. "No cell phones, no ear phones, just relationships, relationships, relationships— time as brothers, hiking, exploring a town, and playing the game we all love."

PLAY STRETCH GAMES
EARLY IN THE SEASON

His British accent only adds to his soccer credibility, with the boys as well as with inquisitive journalists. Assistant Coach Harry Sherwood, Reitnour's right-hand-man since 2011, is unwavering on this point: "Wesleyan plays the toughest schedule it can. There's no point in scheduling weak competition to build an undefeated record. You have to play teams that are better than you."

There's an inherent, inescapable logic to this. Playing stretch competition early in the season identifies the holes you have to fill, while you still have time to fill them. It also shows the coaching staff whom they can trust with those critical post-season minutes.

In fact, back in the Sanford era they would typically enter a tough, mid-season tournament—another overnight away from home—to experience the very format they'd later see in the Final Four. They'd also cross state lines, traveling as far as New Mexico, to duel with nationally-ranked programs Stretch competition, rather than the undefeated season, has always been the better strategy for Wesleyan.

PRINCIPLE 8

TRAIN THEMATICALLY WITH INCREASING COMPLEXITY

When the coaches visited Holland in the 1990s, they observed that the Dutch run many of the same drills across all age levels. From the eight-year-olds to the national team, the training templates were parallel.

For decades now, Wesleyan has adopted a similar, progressive approach. Consider their turning sequence. A drill of standard turns (half, Dutch, three-touch, etc.) progresses to turns with time pressure. Then they add checking your shoulder and shouting the cone color being held up behind you. Repetition builds skills; increasing complexity links it to the match. It's the science of soccer.

What gets trained? They draw their "themes" from the NSCAA "Attacking Principles of Play" and "Defending Principles of Play," time-honored and comprehensive curricula. Lately, about 10 percent are defensive sessions, 20 percent focus on transitions, and the rest r the technical building blocks.

Their 55-page Player Manual—itself a testament to calculation and craftsmanship—sums it up nicely: "We strive for increasing complexity…as we progress through each training session, week and season." In a world where soccer coaches agonize over what to train and how to train it, Wesleyan's Dutch-inspired design—traditional themes and systematic progression—offers an elegant model.

RECALIBRATE TRAINING DURING THE POST-SEASON

In one sense, post-season prep is no different than regular season prep at Wesleyan. They've been preparing for the playoffs all year long. "Aspiring to the highest possible standard is, more than anything else, what propelled us to sustained success," claims founding coach David Sanford. His teams were never blinded by the shine of last year's trophy.

"Every game," he continues, "we came to give our best. We were our own standard. So when it came to the post-season and championship game, we didn't have to juice ourselves up. We had been doing that for months."

It's an echo of Sun Tzu: "Every battle is won before it is fought." But there is some recalibration. Sanford recalls that every post-season he would shift from a "developmental" mindset to a "performance" mindset: "I was done teaching. Now we had to rehearse and perform."

Rehearsal meant just what it means for an actor or a pianist—practice over and over again exactly what's going to happen on stage. For Sanford, that boiled down to shadow play, set pieces, and defensive shape, making every drill as competitive as possible. Simplicity is beautiful.

In the Reitnour era, he too simplifies to what's primary for post-season, but equally important (something he gleaned from Sanford) is managing mindset. The practice before the first playoff game, for example, is largely a sit-in-a-circle powwow where the seniors offer personal reflections. They speak from the gut about three questions: What are you going to miss the most, what's the fondest memory of your career, and what advice do you have for the underclassmen?

Says Reitnour, it has the effect of making everyone care even more about tomorrow. They desperately want to continue playing together. It also forms the nucleus of his post-season team talks.

Psychology speaks louder than X's and O's at this point, and the results speak for themselves.

PRINCIPLE 10

FOCUS THE TEAM THROUGH PRE-GAME PREP

Execution born of focus. And plenty of time together. That's the secret recipe for peak performance on match day in this program.

For away matches, lengthy bus rides through the rural Carolina hills provide that platform. Some of the trip is a silent study hall; some involves team activities. None of it involves ear buds or iPhones.

Preparation for home matches follows the same focus principle, but it's even more orchestrated—almost an art form. Immediately after school there's study hall in coach's classroom from 3:21 to 3:58. Uncommon numbers prompt precision. Next there's the team meal in the cafeteria; then back to the classroom where blaring music welcomes everyone to some hang out time. They play a couple games that have nothing to do with soccer, they dress, they have a brief team chapel and some private "focus time" to get centered. A few words from the coach and then it's out to the field: two lines, hand-in-hand, not a word.

They invest nearly *four hours* together—another half of a school day—before a home match that begins at 7 p.m. (on Saturdays, it's closer to six hours together). Clearly unusual. Some might say excessive. So I asked the roundtable of coaches I was interviewing: "Why not, like most high schools, just send the kids home at 3:00 and have them show up fresh an hour before kickoff?" Their disgust was unanimous, even palpable. An awkward pause, then a chorus of "no." Just no. One terse, dismissive syllable each. That's clearly not The Wesleyan Way.

Going to battle with their brothers requires prolonged preparation—focused and *collective* preparation. Team time builds anticipation. It builds adrenaline. Beyond that, their longstanding pre-game traditions—the team meal, the songs they sing, the sign they slap entering the field, the bagpipes summoning over the speakers—remind these teenagers that they're part of something bigger than themselves. It fuels what Coach Sanford calls "a championship mindset in every game." When they finally step across the line at 7:00, it's the culmination of a highly-choreographed process. They're ready to execute with excellence.

PRINCIPLE 11

BE RELENTLESS ON BOTH SIDES
OF THE BALL

You could call them FC Relentless. At least that seems to be their vision. Out of possession, swarm and suffocate. In possession, attack in numbers. And they'll often add a touch of anarchy, releasing special players to interpret space and create chaos.

The indoctrination begins in elementary school. Say to any WISL participant "we are nothing" and he or she will instantly reply "without the ball." Say to them "split second" and they'll reply "six seconds"—that is, react in a split second to losing possession and regain the ball (with a quick nod toward Barcelona) within six seconds. Years later as varsity players, the onslaught philosophy is now part of their DNA. Their 12-month fitness standards make the execution possible.

But why a predominantly attacking approach when everybody knows that "defense wins titles"? For one thing, they've seen how it wears down teams. For another, they prefer what's aesthetically pleasing. Nobody at Wesleyan wants to grind things out with preventative, reactive, minimalistic tactics, even when holding a lead.

Most importantly, though, if you ask the head coach: "We're going to play a high press and accelerate the game and keep scoring because it gets Number Two and Number Three on the field." More goals means more playing time for everyone. Relentlessness develops reserves … which points to their final principle of performance.

PREPARE FOR NEXT SEASON THIS SEASON

There are no rebuilding years at Wesleyan. Not since 2003 at least. And that's by delicious design.

As we just saw, their style of play—incessant attack to create distance on the scoreboard—gets their second and third units on the field. It's on-the-job training in preparation for next season. Of the 26 or 27 rostered for varsity, 20 of them will play regularly. Sometimes it's a risk. Reitnour admits that they may even lose a game every now and then because they play so deeply, but over the long haul the strategy helps them sustain success.

Makes sense to coaches; doesn't always make sense to the best players on the team who are only logging 55 minutes. But they get it eventually. They learn the wisdom of preparing for next season this season.

In fact, that seems to be the guiding, gilded metaphor for the entire program. The youth instruction prepares them for middle school which prepares them for varsity. Drill One prepares them for Drill Two. Stretch games prepare them for title games. Through it all, they're being prepared for life as "men built for others."

The Wesleyan Way may be 12 principles 12 months a year, but ultimately it works so well because the coaches take an even more transcendent view.

APPENDICES

A. Wesleyan Instructional Soccer League (WISL)

B. "Wesleyan Wednesdays"

C. "Sports Ministry Training" Curriculum

D. Fitness Assessments and Exercises

E. Technical and Tactical Training: Coach Reitnour's Favorite Drills

F. Off-Season Soccer Events

WESLEYAN INSTRUCTIONAL SOCCER LEAGUE (WISL)

This weekly training for Wesleyan elementary school children runs every Wednesday from 2:30 to 4:30, early March through early May. Students are organized into teams, each of which bears the name of a famous international club or national side. The final week of training is dedicated to playoffs among the top teams.

A typical session looks like this:

- 2:30-3:15 Change clothes, then warm up with a kids versus coaches possession game. A coach tracks time of possession to determine a winner. Up to 100 kids play against six coaches on a full field.
- 3:15-3:30 Technical training: games include relays, rooster tag, tree tag, sharks and minnows, and 1v1 ladder, among others.
- 3:30-3:45 Game 1. Foci include compactness, immediate chase, width and depth, keeping the ball, triangle and diamond shapes, passing on the ground, pass and move.
- 3:45-4:00 Sports ministry training (same topics as listed in Appendix C).
- 4:00-4:15 Game 2
- 4:15-4:30 Clean up and dismissal

"WESLEYAN WEDNESDAYS"

On Wednesdays during the season, in lieu of their regular training, all of the boys' teams—90 players representing varsity, JV and middle school—come together for pool training. Across several stations that focus on different skill sets, integrated groups engage in technical training requiring them to "see, think, communicate and execute" all in the same moment.

They run much of the varsity training curriculum, watered down a bit, with the sixth grader playing alongside the twelfth grader. Here is a typical training session:

- 3:30-3:40 All players work on a "ball mastery series" (various technical skills, progressively adding pace and head-up vision)
- 3:40-4:20 In mixed groups of 10-12 (each group is given an English Premier League club name), participants rotate across eight stations. Varsity players remain with one station to run the training. Topics include 1v1 attacking, turning, speed of play, combinations, receiving flighted balls, and finishing.
- 4:20-4:50 9v9 games with integrated teams (varsity guys are to work hard but they are not allowed to initiate contact). Conditions are placed on the boys that replicate what the coaches want to see in the match environment (e.g. touch restrictions, pass and sprint, etc.).
- 4:50-5:00 Sports ministry training, with each group led by a varsity player. For topics, see Appendix C.

"Sports Ministry Training" Curriculum

"Sports ministry" basically means using athletics as a platform for inreach and outreach, and it's at the core of the transformational mission of Wesleyan Christian Academy. The following are representative topics and discussion questions covered at the end of "Wesleyan Wednesdays" and in the WISL program, but the themes also transcend the program.

Identity / Significance
- Where do you place your identity?
- Where should your identity be?
- What are ways you can guard against these false identities?
- Scriptural teaching: Philippians 3:4-7

Competition
- What is competition?
- How has competition negatively impacted you?
- Does knowing that competition means "striving together" change your view?
- What should competition mean?
- Scriptural teaching: Romans 12:1-2

Motivation
- What are your motivations in life, soccer, etc.?
- What should motivate us?
- What are you working towards and how should that motivate you?
- Scriptural teaching: Colossians 3: 17, 23

Gamesmanship
- What is gamesmanship?
- What are common forms of gamesmanship?
- Why are these wrong?

- Is it worth compromising your integrity just to win?
- Scriptural teaching: Joshua 7

Emotions
- What emotions are typically felt during a game?
- What are positive and negative emotions?
- How should you react when a cheap shot is taken, you lose playing time, etc.?
- What emotions are the hardest for you?
- Scriptural teaching: Luke 22:22, 47-51

Taming the Tongue
- Why should you tame the tongue?
- Can you recall a time when a teammate was detrimental to the team because he failed to tame his tongue?
- How does failure to tame your tongue affect our environment?
- How does it affect spectators, kids, and parents?
- How can we be proactive in taming our tongues?
- Scriptural teaching: Psalm 34:13; Proverbs 10:19; James 3:1-12

Respect for Authorities
- Why is it important to respect authorities?
- Has it ever been hard to respect someone in authority? Why?
- What are ways that can help in respecting authorities?
- Scriptural teaching: 1 Samuel 24

Servant Attitude
- What is a servant attitude? Why is it important?
- What happens when everyone is only looking out for themselves?
- How does a team of servants positively affect the environment?
- How can you become a servant?
- Scriptural teaching: Mark 10:35-45; Philippians 2:5-11

Unity
- What is unity?
- How have you seen a lack of unity destroy a team?
- Have you been on a team with unity that helped make the team better?
- What are practical ways that we can become unified?
- Scriptural teaching: 1 Corinthians 12:12-27

Pride (i.e., arrogance, self-centeredness)
- Where in your life do you struggle with pride?
- How does pride affect you and those around you?
- What is humility and why is so important?
- Is there an appropriate form of pride?
- Scriptural teaching: John 15:1-5; 1 Corinthians 10:31

Encouragement
- What is encouragement? And why is it important?
- What is negative about not being encouraging?
- What are the benefits and forms of encouragement?
- Scriptural teaching: Colossians 3:12-17

Imago Dei Soccer Academy

Wesleyan coaches also run a year-round sports ministry, in conjunction with Missionary Athletes International. The Imago Dei Soccer Academy offers high-level, customized skills training for elite elementary through collegiate soccer players, many of whom attend Wesleyan Academy. But it's primary purpose is "to encourage participants, who are 'made in the Image of God,' to utilize their gifts, talents and abilities—specifically in the game of soccer—to glorify God. Pursuing excellence in the game of soccer is the point of Imago Dei; glorifying God with our talents is our purpose." More information is available at www.imagodeisoccer.com.

FITNESS ASSESSMENTS AND EXERCISES

Quarterly Assessments

Fitness assessments occur in November, January, and May: Set the treadmill at 12.0 and run for as long as you can. Also, players do as many pull-ups and push-ups as they can, and complete an Illinois Agility Test in a 5x10 square. Their August pre-season assessment is a timed 1.5 mile run with the standard being nine minutes. All assessment results are tracked throughout a player's career and publicly posted on the coach's classroom door.

Two Staples of Wesleyan's Fitness Training

The SPX Training Series is adopted from the boys' soccer program at Saint Pius X High School (i.e., SPX) in Albuquerque, New Mexico. Each set of sprints follows the previous set, after a 60 second break, so that one training session is comprised of 70 sprints (18+16+14+12+10).

- 18 x 20s: Sprint 20 yards. Rest 15 seconds. Complete 18 repetitions.
- 16 x 40s: Sprint 40 yards. Rest 20 seconds. Complete 16 repetitions.
- 14 x 60s: Sprint 60 yards. Rest 30 seconds. Complete 14 repetitions.
- 12 x 80s: Sprint 80 yards. Rest 45 seconds. Complete 12 repetitions.
- 10 x 120s: Sprint 120 yards. Rest 60 seconds. Complete 10 repetitions.

The Hartwick Training Series is fitness training with a ball. Wesleyan adapted their current sequence of drills from North Carolina State's soccer curriculum. To complete the entire series takes about 45 minutes.

Ball Control and Agility

4 minutes	Jog while executing Coerver** moves, with quick touches, changing direction and speed. Complete as many moves as possible.
1 minute	Head juggle
4 minutes	Jog while executing Coerver moves, then explode for 5-8 yards on the final touch. Accelerate away after each move.
1 minute	Thigh juggle
1 minute	Throw ball in air and then head trap the ball to your feet. On the trap, accelerate 5-10 yards into space.
1 minute	Foot juggle with no spin on the ball
1 minute	Throw ball in the air, thigh trap and then accelerate 5-8 yards into space
1 minute	Sit-ups
1 minute	Throw ball in the air, trap with feet and then accelerate 8-10 yards into space
2 minutes	Total body juggle
4 minutes	Sit down, throw the ball in the air, trap with either foot, accelerate 8-10 yards into space
4 minutes	Sit down, throw the ball in the air, jump and head or chest trap the ball, accelerate 5-8 yards into space
2 minutes	Crunches
2 minutes	Jog around field

Technical Speed, Pure Speed and Endurance

Figure 8s	Place two cones 15 yards apart. Dribble the ball in a Figure 8 pattern around the cones. Start with a long touch towards the first cone, accelerating with the first touch, then quick touches around the cone. Do this 3 times using the inside of the right foot, 3 times using the outside of the right foot, 3 times using the inside of the left foot, and 3 times using the outside of the left foot.
Rest	Walk for 30 seconds
Shuttles	Place two cones 10 yards apart. Shuffle 10 times from side to side using a slide step.
Rest	Walk for 30 seconds
Jumps	Place two cones 10 yards apart. Two legged explosive jumps (bounds), up and back three times. Then one legged explosive hops three times up and back with the right leg. Then one legged explosive hops three times up and back with the left leg.
Rest	Walk for 30 seconds
Passing	Place two cones 25 yards apart. Pass the ball from one cone to the other, sprint to the ball. If the ball does not make it to the cone, drop down where the ball is and do 25 sit-ups. Collect the ball and sprint dribble to the starting line. Make five passes and then take a 15 second break. Repeat the entire series three times.

Strength and Flexibility

Jumps	60 jumps over the ball forward and backwards with both feet together
Rest	Do 15 Figure 8s by standing with legs spread apart and knees straight. Roll the ball with your hands in a Figure 8 pattern around your legs.
Jumps	60 jumps over the ball from side to side
Rest	Do 15 roll arounds. Sit with your legs straight out and roll the ball around the soles of your feet.
Jumps	Throw the ball in the air, jump and then touch the ball back up in the air (as if you were setting a volleyball) before your feet hit the ground. Repeat 60 times.
End	20 push-ups and 30 sit-ups

** Coerver moves and ball mastery skills derive from the philosophy and methodology of championship Dutch coach Wiel Coerver, who in the 1970s and 80s developed a system for individual skill development that remains popular to this day. Any Google or YouTube search will provide a wealth of examples.

TECHNICAL AND TACTICAL TRAINING: COACH REITNOUR'S FAVORITE DRILLS

4v4 Arsenal

- Play 4v4 inside a grid that's 27 wide by 30 long. Pass to any of four target players in either end zone to score a point. For the first stage, end zone targets are static and get one or two touches, playing back to their own team after a goal.
- Progress to replacing target players in the end zone: Progression 1 is replacement by the passer. Progression 2 is replacement by someone other than the passer who is near the end zone.
- For Progression 3, the head coach in the middle of the grid holds up a colored cone and a team gets a bonus point if a player receiving the ball first checks his shoulder for the color and calls it out.
- Some objectives include: ball on the ground, split defenders and play second (higher) targets whenever possible, penetration—score if you can or play the longest ball possible, keep shape of triangles and diamonds, think in terms of "penetration, support and mobility."

Team Trains a Keeper

- 3v3 or 4v4 in the box with a keeper. To start play, a ball is served in from one of four locations around the corners of the box (representing winger and wingback service). Servers must take a touch, making a Coerver move before serving. Teams play until a goal is scored or the ball is saved, cleared or crosses the end line.

- Service alternates as follows: Every other ball into the box is a shot from the top of the arc, with the ball live after a save or block (so the sequence is service-shot-service-shot, etc.) The coaches' mantra is "frame, follow, finish."
- Coaches keep score; players rotate (offense to defense; inside the box to outside the box) after two rounds of serves.
- Different assistant coaches observe and direct the defenders, attackers and goalkeeper.

Mourinho Triangles (adapted from the training methods of Jose Mourinho)

- Several players train in a Dutch diamond (play is to the right and to the left, two-touch with a three-touch Cruyff option, splits, backside balls, brisk speed of play).
- Adjacent, along one side of the diamond, three players, take positions representing high players (e.g., attacking mid and two forwards, or two holding mids and an attacking mid). Without a ball, they practice their movements to space that they would make based on where the ball is in the Dutch diamond. For them, the diamond represents the lower players on the field and their job is to practice showing for them.
- Along the opposite side of the diamond, players pass one-touch in a triangle, based on a coach-determined passing pattern (this part of the drill is not dependent on what is happening in the other two parts.)
- After two minutes, players rotate among the three stations. Typically they go two full rotations, or 12 minutes.

Wesleyan W Passing (adapted from a training methods of Dave Brandt). Five players are organized into a W formation: one target player up top (back to the goal), two wingers and two supporting players who could represent mids or outside backs. Players pass and move based on a pattern determined by the coach, training options that fit their system. Among the patterns that Wesleyan uses are:

- **Basic:** The five players move the ball in a W. The ball stays on the ground and is always received across the body. Wingers can check away and use a three-touch Cruyff option. Speed of play is paramount.
- **"Give-Go Target"** trains the option of a give-go between the winger and target. After the winger receives the wall pass, he takes it across his body, Cruyffs and plays his support who plays the target and the pattern continues on the other side of the W.
- **"Give-Go Support"** trains the option of a give-go between a support player and a winger. The wing then Cruyffs and plays his support again who plays the target and the pattern continues on the other side of the W.
- **"Find the Third Man"** trains the decoy run. The pattern is: supporting player to winger to support to target. The strong side winger then makes a decoy run downfield, calling for the ball but the target turns away and plays weak side support who then plays his winger.
- **"Load Low and Cruyff Split":** Winger checks back very low (to bring defender with him), then sprints to receive ball from his support player. Winger Cruyffs and then plays it back to the support who plays the target and the pattern continues on the other side of the W.
- **"8/10 Presses Through"** trains through runs by the

box-to-box and attacking midfielders (called 8 and 10 in Wesleyan numbering system). The pattern is: midfield supporting player to target who turns away and plays weak side support as the first midfielder sprints past target. Support player hits his winger rather than the runner. Target and overlapping mid switch places to continue the flow of the drill.

- **"Slip"** trains a through ball to an overlapping midfielder. The pattern is this: As a mid receives the ball in a support position, the target checks toward him and the weak side mid sprints into the space behind the target. The ball is played to the runner who then Cruyffs and plays the strong side winger who plays support (formerly the target player). Target and mid switch places to continue the flow of the drill.

- **"Seven"** trains player exchange and the long switch. The pattern is: support player to strong side winger who Cruyffs and plays back to support. The weak side winger checks inside, the weak side support player overlaps into the space behind him and receives the switched ball. Players are asked to visualize this as a winger/outside back exchange. He Cruyffs and plays support (formerly the winger who has exchanged spots to continue the flow of the drill).

- **"Overlap":** Support player hits his winger and overlaps around him. Winger takes a touch inside and plays the target who plays weak side support. Support and winger exchange spots to continue the flow of the drill.

- **"Player's Choice":** Options reside with players, staying within the principles of play set by the coach.

- **"One Touch":** This runs as the name implies.

- **5v3 then 5v4:** Defenders are added with a large goal and keeper behind the W and two small goals on the other end. The W patterns are trained under pressure.

Robbins Transition W's: Named for former Wesleyan player and current Assistant Coach, Carter Robbins who invented important parts of it, this shadow drill trains quick organization and correct shape in positive and negative transitions. Eleven players in their usual positions on a full field await one of three prompts from the coach:

- When the coach holds up a red cone, that means Wesleyan has just lost possession and needs to get compact in its defensive half.
- When the coach holds up a yellow cone, it means Wesleyan has just won possession and needs to expand. They are essentially in the shape of two W's at this point, one high and one low, and in a match they would leverage the W patterns described in the previous drill.
- When the coach holds up a green cone, it means Wesleyan has penetrated into the attacking third and, among other things, one of the centerbacks needs to step higher in support of the attack, creating a three-back system.

Messiah-Sherwood Finishing: Named for Messiah College soccer and Assistant Coach Harry Sherwood, the innovators of this sequence, this is a finishing drill with keepers and full-size goals set 36 yards apart, four players in lines behind each of the four posts, and a few flank players awaiting serves on the sideline at the midfield stripe. All players at a goal are on the same team, as is the winger to whom they serve the ball. There are three variations:

- **2v0 Drill:** Ball gets served from a player at the right post to his winger on the right. The server and one of his teammates sprint toward the opposite goal to get on the end of a cross from the winger. Wingers alternate between "clean-and-cross" and "seven ball" serves. Players in the box get a maximum of one touch each to score. Then the opposite team serves to their winger and the play continues at the other end.

- **3v1 Drill:** Same drill except three players attack the goal, with one from the opposite team defending in the box. The attacking player who takes the shot becomes the defender at the opposite end as play switches.

- **4v2 Drill:** Same drill except with four attackers and two defenders. In both this and the 3v1 version, wingers have to pick out intentional targets and attackers have to make intentional and coordinated runs.

Off Season Soccer Events

During the off-season, the Wesleyan coaches organize several soccer events for students, parents and Wesleyan employees and alumni. This is part of creating "the best environment in the state to play soccer" (Principle 3). These are the major off-season activities:

November and December

Open gym futsal two nights each week. This activity draws up to 90 participants per night, including employees and alumni.

January

The Wesleyan Indoor Soccer Tournament takes place on a Saturday, with dozens of teams competing in both student and adult divisions. Entry fee is $130 per team with a maximum roster of 10. Matches are 18 minutes in length (running clock format), they use a futsal ball, and each team is guaranteed at least three matches throughout the day.

February

Wesleyan partners with the Charlotte Eagles professional team (www.charlotteeagles.com) to organize a five-hour indoor tournament for "non-athletic regular people," abbreviated as NARP Fest. The stated purpose of the event is "to enjoy an evening of food, fun and fellowship with our school community and our Charlotte Eagles friends." Participants also bring new or gently used soccer gear and equipment to donate to the Eagles urban outreach ministry. The $25 team registration fee also goes to the Eagles ministry. Rosters are co-ed, with a maximum of one varsity boy and one varsity girl per team. Games are 8v8, with a champion crowned at the end of the night. Food is provided by Fellowship of Christian Athletes and participants hear a few public testimonies during the meal time.

March through May

Each spring, seventh to twelfth grade students, as well as some quality adult players from the Wesleyan Academy community, participate in a 7v7 league that they call "Bundesliga." About 80 players get drafted onto six teams, all of which bear German club names, and they play 30-minute matches after school every Wednesday, with kickoffs at 4:30, 5:00 and 5:30. Each player wears a tee-shirt representing the colors of his or her German club.

The coaches meticulously track player statistics and they award a golden boot, a silver boot and a golden glove at the same time that they crown a league champion in May.

June and July

In June, they run a weeklong camp for elementary school players during the day and for middle school and high school players in the evening, with about 100 participants in each session. Coaches for the camp include not just the Wesleyan coaches, but also top college players and some pro players and college coaches who are in the network of the Wesleyan leadership.

In July they run their "Program Camp" for Wesleyan rising

sixth through twelfth graders. Alumni also come in to train alongside of the varsity players. This four-day camp at the school is a day camp for middle schoolers and a sleepover camp for JV and varsity.

MICHAEL ZIGARELLI, Ph.D., is a professor at Messiah College in Pennsylvania and the author of twelve books, most of which focus on leadership and organizational performance. His other coaching books include *The Messiah Method* and *Soccer Field, Mission Field.* You can reach him at mzigarelli@messiah.edu

Made in the USA
Middletown, DE
23 July 2017